My Shade of Colors

When Will This Dark Cloud End?

DEDICATION:

This book is dedicated to the one and only: "Paul Elzey." I never knew a stranger who choose to sit next to me at a local bar and insist for me to tell him everything that was on my mind. After having that one long conversation he had this crazy idea of me writing a book about my life. God has blessed me and sent me an angel who believed in me when I didn't acknowledge the gift I really had inside. So Paul I have to say; no I didn't give up and without you this book wouldn't be here. Thank you and hopefully we can bump into each other again. God bless!

THANK YOU MESSAGE:

I want to thank all the readers who took time out to read my story. This book was written to help young adults in the world. No matter what I want you to know that you are not alone and there is always someone out there that has it worst. So in that being said never give up on your dream, because if you don't try you won't have!
Love...Phylisia Slim

Special Thanks:

To all my family and friends. Especially to Rob, Bobby Prince, Robert Philizaire,

And most of all My Father Up Above

MY SHADE OF COLORS:

WHEN WILL THIS DARK CLOUD END?

PROLOGUE 4

BRONX LIFE.. 9

LIFE IS ABOUT CHANGES 23

FLORIDA HERE I COME ....…............ 29

SUICIDE ....…..... 39

GUARDIAN ANGEL 49

MEDICINE FOR THE BRAIN ....…............ 54

WELCOME MYSTERY MAN TO THE FAMILY.... 59

EDUCATION IS THE KEY 63

LOVE IS PAIN 73

SEX TO REALITY 82

SURPRISES MEANT FOR A LIFETIME 89

WHAT'S LOVE?" 95

THE EYE THAT BLEEDS............................…..101

YOU HAVE THE RIGHT TO REMAIN SILENT...109

"PROLOGUE"

"Daddy! Stop! Get off of her! You are hurting her! Stop hitting her! Mommy, are you okay?"

"See how you so fucking evil! I can't believe you fighting me off in front of our daughter".

Looking at the way dad was beating up mom, I had to do something. Even though I tried to use all my strength to pull him off of her it didn't matter. Right when he was about to give mom one more hit...he said:

"You lucky Phylisia here".

He turned around with tears in his eyes, and just gave me a hug and said. "I'm sorry baby doll but I want you to always remember no matter what your mother says your daddy's little girl, daddy will always love you".

The way I was mad at him I didn't know if he was even telling the truth. "Okay daddy, can you and mommy stop fighting now? Daddy can I please be alone with mommy right now?"

Looking at the way dad just walked out the room and slam the door, I didn't know that you can feel relief and sad at the same time.

See mom and dad been having a lot of issues lately, which means a lot of fights. I try my best to not get in the middle of their fights because of course it wasn't none of my business, but tonight was different. Let's just say I had enough! Mom face looks so hurt in every way, seeing what happened just now I knew she wasn't okay.

"Mommy, can I talk to you?"

The way she looked at me, I could tell she didn't want to talk.

"I'm sorry you had to see that Phylisia, but I'm alright".

"Mommy I'm nine years old not three; so I know you're not alright. I just have to tell you something, I don't want you and daddy together anymore. He's hurting you too much."

"Phylisia, I'm fine now, just go to bed."

Leaving my mom's room and not knowing what's going to happen next, was one of the hardest thing for me to do. While walking to my pink room to go to bed, tears just started to fall. I just couldn't stop crying; my family was breaking apart. Why are they always fighting?

How could my three younger sisters sleep through it? I love my dad, but I hate it when he beat on my mom. I couldn't just go to sleep after all that drama; so I had to talk to god first.

"Dear God, who's in heaven. Please help my family, but most of all help my mom. In Jesus name I pray, Amen".

Even though I wanted a nice happy family, but somewhere in my nine years old mind; I knew that wouldn't be.

"Phylisia, get up you have to go to school."

"Okay mom I'm up."

Waking up the next morning I knew I didn't want to go anywhere. After what happen last night I didn't want to leave mom's side. Right when I was trying to get ready, quietly that's when I heard dad's mouth. "Kids come here, daddy need to talk to you all".

Listening to those words I knew this wasn't going to be good. Walking downstairs with my sisters in which they all had smiles on their faces, unlike myself who knew the hidden truth. The only thing that was on my mind was finding out if I was going to lose the one man in my life. That's when dad grab us close with a big smile on his face.

"Good morning daddy's little girls, I wonder if you girls dream about me last night?"

I couldn't believe the way dad was acting like nothing happen last night.

"Listen up girls, daddy going to be out of town for a while. I want all of you girls to behave yourself, alright? Remember daddy love his girls".

I watched how dad gave a kiss to my younger sisters; Kelly-Ann,

who's seven, Vanesia, who's two and last but not least was Shanice, who's one. Finally, he gave me a kiss good bye.

"Alright, Phylisia and Kelly-Ann its school time, so let's get going".

A lot of things were running through my mind, like good things, but also bad things. I didn't know what was going to happen now that dad was gone. Mom doesn't spend time with us like how dad do because she is always working. I knew we weren't going to see dad for a while. Now, I have to say this is when my dark cloud began.

"Falling Steps"

It's what you call pain, but at the same time it can be what you been asking for

The tears that would fall from your eyes, from all the hurtful things you went through

Knowing you didn't have to, but you couldn't control yourself from knowing what's good for you to what may be wrong

People giving you warnings, but you not trying to listen

Instead, you just letting one word come in one ear, and out the other

Through all the madness you not knowing that it would one day be all sadness

Sadness for you to just wish you can just close your eyes and never wakeup again.

Years Later.......

"Bronx Life"

"Phylisia get up! Tell me how you could go to bed when dishes dem in the sink!"

"So you woke me up early in the morning, knowing I have to go to school in the next couple of hours, just so I can wash some damn dishes?"

" Don't fucking back chat me, after I'm the one that been on my fucking legs all day, working to put food in yah damn belly!"

"Okay whatever you say…"

This shit is bullshit! One fucking cup in the sink, and two plates, was it that serious?

Damn, in the next five hours I have to go to school, that's if I go. Ever since dad left it was like the world was on my shoulder, I was now fourteen years old and life wasn't getting any easier for me.

"Hurry up you have to go to school."

"Okay mom I'm up!"

Fuck that shit I'm not going to no damn school today; they can survive without me.

Walking out the house I just wasn't in the mood for those teachers. So I figure to call my home girl up to see what she was up to.

"Shayne! Where you at girl, I'm not going to school today, so where we going to meet at?"

"Slimazz, what happen to you last night?"

"You know who as usual, can you believe she fucking woke me up early in the fucking morning! To wash some damn dishes! Like damn, why can't she give me some credit, after all, I'm the one that be staying home with her damn kids every day!"

" Slimazz, that's your mom, but anyways meet me on 215 & Bronx wood". Growing up in the Bronx, New York my name on the block was Slimazz, which usually the Jamaicans would call me or even Slim for the Americans, neither really didn't make a difference for me.

Walking to the block, I try my best not to think about my mom.

"Sexy Slimazz can I come talk to you?"

This tall, light skin guy that wasn't my type wanted to talk to me. I didn't mind because I needed someone that would show me some love anyways.

"Nobody stopping you right?"

Look at this guy, he didn't look that bad, but let's see what he has.

"Hey, what's up I see you was looking hard".

"I couldn't help myself, you beautiful", he said.

"Thank you babes, how about you give me your number and I'll call you". "I'm going to give you my number, but you better call me".

"Alright cutie". Sometimes you got to say things to make a nigga feel good. Yeah, I was searching for comfort, but not a relationship. I didn't like no man claiming me, I was already getting stress out at home.

"Ring, Ring" Yeah that was Shayne calling me now.

"I see u, stay right there". I knew Shayne since I was in third grade, so we were very close.

"Girl, tell me how I got a new number in my phone book."

"Slimazz, you crazy, sooner or later your phonebook can't hold anymore". To me playing around with guy's head was my hobby. These guys be doing the same thing to these ladies, so I just choose to run the same game on them.

"Anyways, Slimazz what do u got plan out for today?"

"Well, I wanted to meet up with somebody, let's see who's free."

"You know that won't be hard, Slimazz".

See for a fourteen-year-old I was very mature for my age. I didn't blend in too well with females. They were always a problem, so I had a lot of male friends. There was a time when I would go to school and come straight home, but that was when the kids (my sisters) were too young to take care of themselves. Before I continue, like two years ago when I was only twelve years old, rumors started. See, my mom is a nurse and also a hairdresser, so she was very popular. She owned her own hair & nail shop on East Gun Hill Rd. Sometimes I would be at the shop, in which I had to help my mom out with customers. Across the street was Evander Childs High School, which was the worst school in the Bronx. Of course I look mature for my age, so guys started looking and I didn't know females had problems with me. So rumors start to spread, and my mom would come home and called me every name in the book. I guess she believe what she heard, but at the same time I didn't know what she was talking about. Like how can I be a whore if I never had sex? All this drama was going on for a good two years, until I finally gave up. I gave up on everything, and everybody. I wasn't getting the love from my mother, in fact she was my enemy that would come home every night and curse me out. So the only choice I had was to take the heat. So finally I was curious to know what sex was about, and how it felt. That's when the coldhearted Slimazz came out, if I couldn't get love from my own mother I wasn't expected it from no one else.

Now that I made all that clear I'm going to head back to my day. Standing next to Shayne and scolding down my phonebook I knew I would find someone to chill with.

"Okay girl let's call Richie."

"Is that the guy from that party Saturday night last weekend?"

"Yea, the one that was buying us drinks all night... he was cute".

"I'm calling, let's see what's up with him." It didn't take long for Richie to answer his phone.

"Who this?"

"Well hello cutie, this is Slimazz."

"Hey baby girl, I'm surprise you call me, I have been waiting a good week to hear your sexy voice."

See this is how guys talk when they want something, nice and sweet like you're the only girl in their eyes, yea right, but them not knowing what they getting themselves into. You know what they say: It takes a player to know one.

"Well I guess you're happy to hear from me, so what do you have plan out for us, sweetie?"

In their eyes I was a regular innocent slim girl, that they thought they could just walk all over.

"Actually, I'm just home bored, what you coming through?"

"That would be fine, but I want you to know that I'm not alone."

"Oh, so you telling me you with your second half, you know I don't have anyone that would want to link up with her."

"Yes I'm with my home girl, and that's okay we can just chill."

"You funny, you know that's not going to happen, but I will make sure I have your bailey's drink here waiting on you."

"Okay babes, later."

See, one thing about me I knew people would talk shit about my home girl all the time, talking about her weight, but she always been there for me. So I couldn't care less, after I'm not the one fucking her.

"So what happen girl?"

"Yea, we going by his crib, what you really think he would let all of this go? Plus, he got my drink over there, so you know he want it bad."

Walking toward his door and giving it a knock we didn't know what to expect.

"Yea girl we going to see how clean this motherfucker is."

It took him a good minute to open the door like he wasn't finish straighten up his place. See I have a thing about older guys, yea I was only 14, but who cares. Richie, was 21 years old with a job, car, and most of all his own crib, so ladies I know you like those independent man.

"Hey, baby sorry I took so long."

"That's alright boo, so you already met my friend Shayne."

"Yea I did, hey Shayne."

"Hello to you too, she said."

"So ladies y'all can come in."

Walking in his place I couldn't help but say... damn!

This guy was really into art, he had pictures all over his walls, carpet clean, yea he was doing his thing.

"Well nice spot, I really do like."

"Thank you Slimazz the only thing missing is my queen, just make yourself comfortable."

While we were sitting on the couch watching TV he came from the kitchen with my bailey's in his hands.

"What you thought I was playing, no I know how to treat a lady now, especially when she's mine."

Yea right! I thought he knew I can never be claim.

"So, Shayne would you like some?"

"Oh no thank you, I don't drink."

That was a habit Shayne had, she would always make me look like the bad girl, but she's the same person that finds all this shit entertaining. So Richie came to sit next to me and poured my drink into a glass. While I was sipping my drink he put his arm around my neck, trying my best to ignore him, I smelt something sexy.

"What do you have on?"

"It's Curve, do you like?"

"Oh, yes it is really sexy."

"So let me show you what else is sexy."

Out of nowhere he moves forward and we just starting kissing. Kissing, like we were going to start a movie, we forgot Shayne was right there just watching us.

"Okay, you two need to find a room upstairs, because I don't need to be seeing this."

"Alright...we will be back."

Looking at the way he just picked me up from the couch, I can't lie it was turning me on. We reach upstairs, into his room, and he throw me on the bed. While he was kissing all over me he started telling me what he loves about me.

"Ooh baby I love the way you dance like no one is watching you, with those seductive eyes of yours. I love the way you walk; you are my dream model. I even love your aggressive mouth."

Wow...I couldn't believe this guy, I know he won't be hard, it looks like his already falling. I can tell he loves to use his lips, because the way he went down on me I can tell that he was a pro. The way he handles me was just the way I like it, he made me make love to him, which is my favorite. It didn't take long until I made him cum, of course.

" I'm going to check up on Shayne I'll be back." The way he was relax I could tell he just didn't want to move, which means I did a great job. Main thing that was on my mind was getting my behind downstairs so I can brag about this juicy topic to Shayne.

"Girl, he was telling me some sweet shit, like he loves how I walk, and most of all he loves my mouth, and not in that nasty way!"

"Now you know he lost his damn mind, tell me what fool would love that smart ass mouth of yours, Slimazz."

"I don't know, but all I know is I got him upstairs looking up at the ceiling not moving! See this is why you be hearing my name cause...Slimazz got the good, good! Look, this is a bet I will give him two weeks for him to fall so deep in love with me that he will start calling me at least ten times a day."

"Okay, Slimazz I believe you alright."

"I'll be back I'm going to tell him that I'm leaving, knowing him he better gives me some pocket money." Walking upstairs I knew this would be easy.

"Hey babe I'm about to leave alright, so don't miss me."

"Oh you leaving already? Come here, you know I like to take care of you as my lady.

So here is something for you, maybe you can get more of those sexy panties for the next time I see you."

Me knowing this probably wasn't going to happen anytime soon I just went along with the flow.

"Okay boo, I'll talk to you later."

Giving him a kiss goodbye, I knew it wouldn't be long till I hear from him. "Slimazz, did you get what you want?"

"Girl, what do you think?"

Walking to the shop, I knew I didn't want to see my mom's face, much less hear her voice.

"Phylisia! Come help me pull out this customer braids, then wash and blow out his hair."

One thing about me no matter how much I couldn't stand my mom; I was always there to help her.

"Alright Shayne call me later."

"Yea girl."

The way mom was looking at us I knew she was about to say something smart.

" What would you two do without each other."

Hearing what she said I just couldn't get what she was saying, like I wonder what my mom would do without me. The one and only thing I knew I wanted from my mom was just some love. That was the one problem my mom had, she won't show any love to her kids, she treats us like we came into this world at the wrong time. I guess she was showing us the hard love. Her not knowing that we know that she's going through a lot, but that's when you should show us that everything is going to be alright.

While doing her customer's hair, I just watch how she would act like everything is alright, she looks so happy. Thinking to myself she just acts so fake, but why can't she ever act like that with us? Which only makes me piss the fuck off with her, because when she need help, or even when she's hurting I'm the first person she calls. Then I'm the only one she treats like shit! See I know that my mom loves me, but the kind of love she shows me is the part of love that stings. The part of love like when your stress out, and you just want to come home and take it out on someone. When you don't have no money to pay your bills, and you're wondering where all your money went, and you need someone to blame it on. The entire time I was at the shop I just did my job and didn't speak to her, and that was something she would hate.

"Phylisia, go pull down the shatters!"

I couldn't wait to get home to go to my bed, I had a long day. I went outside to lock up, hoping that I would go home in peace tonight.

"Mom, can I get the car keys, so I can wait in the car?" She and her coworkers was still in the shop talking.

"Here, here take the keys because I wonder why you in a rush for? Tell all your horny man dem that they can wait."

Listening to the way she was talking I could tell she was starting something. Like, I just ask her for the keys why would it move to me rushing her, then to men. Then to make everything worse in front of other people, like they don't have mouths, now that's how rumors start.

Sitting in the car waiting for her, I just started to cry wondering when will she change.

She not knowing that her attitude was just bringing out the anger in me. Anger to the point where I just don't want to be around her anymore.

"Alright ladies later, see you tomorrow."

Looking at the way my mom waved them bye, with a big smile on her face, I just hope I don't hear her mouth. She came in the car and slam the door, started the car. While we were in the car she had to start something.

"Phylisia, tell me why you love to rush me like you're my mother? Are you paying my damn bills?"

See my parents are Jamaican, and one thing they love to do is cuss, which include running their mouths. Everything she was saying I let come in one ear and out the other, because I was just so tired. I lost respect for my mother when she started calling me every name in the book, so me sticking up for myself is something I had to do. We finally reach home and all I could do was get ready for bed.

The morning came, and it was silent in the house. It was a nice Saturday morning, and of course mom had to make money at the shop. So I got up to make something for the kids to eat, while I was doing that my phone was ringing. I look at it and it was Richie, so I ignored the call, but then he called over and over again until I just answer.

"Hey what's up"

"Slimazz, I been calling you, don't you know when your man calling you, you suppose to hurry up and answer."

See this was the reason why I didn't want no man claiming me.

"Look, what did I tell you, you're not my man! Just because I gave you a one fuck doesn't mean I belong to you! I told you I call you when I want some and that's it!"

"You funny Slimazz, you really thing you could just fuck me and that's it? It looks like you got yourself a problem."

"Okay what do you mean by that?"

"I mean you better be careful where you go and what you do, because I said your mine."

I didn't know what to think about that, if that was a threat or if he was just talking shit.

"Listen Richie, I already told you I'm not ready for a relationship."

"Well Slimazz I already have love for you, and I'm not letting no one else take you away from me, like it or not!"

The way he just hung up on me I couldn't believe what I just heard, but anyways he may have been drinking.

"By Time"

How do the winds blow?

How do the water flow?

See it took you awhile to think or did it?

How did that man cry?

How did my clothes dry?

See all you have to do is try.

How did I fell fast asleep, and took a while to awake?

How come that woman's choice was to leave that man, and never have words to explain.

I hope you know what all of this is about, everything happens by time.

"Life Is About Changes"

It was a nice sunny Saturday morning, so I figure to give daddy a call.

"Hey dad, what's up with you today?"

"Well that's a surprise, you made my day feel much better hearing from you."

"So how Florida treating you?"

"Real nice, hopefully one of these days you and the kids can pay me a visit. So how you and your mother doing, I hope you behaving yourself."

"You know the usual, she still stressing me out. I think I need a break from her for a while, so I'm coming to stay with you."

"Phylisia, now you know if you come by me you have to behave yourself okay?" "Alright, dad I shouldn't have a reason not to, but I'm going to talk to you later cause I'm going to make some breakfast for the kids."

"Alright girl, stay good later."

See my father and I have a very special bond, I can talk to him about what's stressing me out and he will always turn it into something positive. My dad may not be a good husband, but I can tell he loves his kids. Dad moved to Florida ever since he packed up and decided mom and him wasn't going to work out. So I have been thinking about just moving away from this place for a while, maybe that's what I need to make mom and I closer. That's when I see mom walking out the door.

"I'm not here, I will be at the shop if you need me."

I knew she wasn't going stay home too long, especially on a Saturday.

While I was cooking breakfast for the kids I was just thinking, maybe moving to Florida would be the best thing for me. I called the kids to come and eat their food, while they were there I figure to talk to them about what I have to do. Yeah I can tell they felt a way, but I had to explain to them that I will always love them and I will always be there for them. Thank god they weren't little babies anymore; Kelly-Ann was twelve, Vanesia was seven and Shanice was six years old now. So in their eyes as long I was happy they would support it. When I was done talking to them I called Shayne up to see what party was going on for tonight.

"Hey girl, what's up for tonight?"

"There's a big bashment party going on, so you know the dancehall

queen Ms. Slimazz have to be there."

"Of course, you know I have to start this party up." One thing about females is they love competition, so because of that I always been the first girl to start dancing then after that the party started.

"Shayne I have to tell you something, I'm going to move by my father."

"Okay, so when you planning on moving?"

"I'm not sure yet."

"Well Slimazz you won't believe who just ask for you."

"Please don't let it be who I think it is."

"Yes Richie! He just drove up behind me, when I was walking to the store and ask me where you were at."

"What you told him?"

"I said I'm not sure, and he just said tell her I'm looking for her."

"I didn't get to tell you what we talked about when he called me, but you could tell I gave him some good good cause he already sprung."

"I could tell by the way he was asking for you, like he was looking for a lost puppy or something."

"He is moving too fast; you know he have the nerve to tell me I belong to him like it or not."

"Slimazz you better be careful, because there is a lot of crazy man over here, it sounds to me like he going to be a big problem."

"I'm not even worrying about him; I will be fine. So I will meet you at your house later on tonight, I'm about to go to the shop and tell mom the good news for me but the bad news for her."

"Slimazz I see you really trying for you and your mom, but good luck alright."

"Alright girl, see you later."

Walking to the shop I try to put myself into my mom shoes. Will she be okay with my idea, or will she just curse me out and say I'm just too ungrateful. I was just going to help out in the shop, and just wait till she's in the good mood to talk. When I reach to the shop I could tell everybody was in a good mood. Mom was playing music, and trying to sing.

"Phylisia come wash out this perm for me."

See I was going to make sure she stays in that mood. So I washed out the customer's hair, while waiting on mom to finish up the customer's hair I just started thinking. I really don't want to leave my home; I know my modeling career would work out better here. Then at the same time I rather my mom and I get closer, instead of her treating me like her enemy.

Soon as the customer left I took a deep breath and just went for it.

"Mom, can I talk to you?"

"Sure, what happen?"

"Well I wanted to know if I could go stay with dad for a while?"

"Now all of a sudden you just want to leave, after I'm the one that been taking care of your black behind! It's alright though your dad stress free, so do what you want. I don't business anymore, and don't come running back to me when nothing works out your way!"

"Mom, I just want to try somewhere new."

See I never told my mom that I was really moving because I wanted us to be closer.

The way she talks to me just make me feel like running into the bathroom to cry, in which I did.

"SHE"

She's the only one I have

She's my soul, my heart, and my nightmare at nights

Yes, she's a pain and sometimes not

But sometimes I have to take it as it goes

Times I look at her and ask myself, why she has to be like that?

Why can't she be more understanding?

I try, I try so hard to talk to her, is she listening to me?

Will she change? I guess not because that she is my mom.

"FLORIDA HERE I COME"

Packing was always hard for me to do, this is something I just hate doing! This is my second year in high school and I surely want to get out of this bad ass school. Now I'm going to be living in the country where the suck up white girls are at. My dad was born and raised in St. Thomas, Jamaica, so he made sure he stays in the country part of Florida. Which is Sarasota county, where it's so quiet, and dead! Ring, ring I wonder who this could be calling me, oh boy, the little trouble maker.

"Yes Richie, how may I help you, I heard you been looking for me?"

"It's simple baby, I just miss you."

"Richie how many times am I going to tell you that we are not together!" "Whatever you say, but all I know is you could like it or not but your mine, you're my lady!"

See this nigga is really scary. I just hung up the phone, I was not going to answer the rest of his calls again. I just call Shayne to tell her the crazy news.

"Shayne, do you know that mad ass man called me, talking about if I like it or not, I'm his."

"See Slimazz, I told you that he was crazy, I guess you gave him too much to handle."

"Funny, so now you got jokes, anyways I'm packing up my clothes and I have this sexy outfit I never wear before. So you know I'm going be on point tonight!"

"Alright Slimazz, meet me at my house midnight."

"Alright girl later."

While I was getting ready to leave I heard mom coming in the house. Damn, I was trying to leave before she came in, now I'm going to hear her mouth.

"Where you think you going at this time of the night?"

"Well, I'm going out with Shayne since I'm about to leave soon."

"See this is your damn problem, you think you too grown to ask me if you could go out!"

"Okay, but you were the one at work all day, and you told me to call you only for emergencies. You the one that's too busy to check up on your kids, cause if you did then I could have told you then."

"Who the fuck you think you talking to like that?"

While she repeated herself again she walked over to me and just gave me a big slap on my face. All I could have done was pick up my bag and just walk out. Walking over to Shayne's I try my best not to think about her, but that was not easy for me to do. "Shayne, I'm outside open the door."

"Slimazz, what happen to you?"

"Nothing, just mom and I had it out."

"As usual, I hope you moving would make things work out for the better." "Yeah, me too, but anyways let's go you know I really need me a drink to get these stress off my mind."

When we reach by the club it was pack, a lot of fine brothers. It didn't take long before one of those fine brothers choose to grab my attention.

"Well, well look what we got here, my name is Jay and yours?"

" Well you could just call me Slim, so Jay what brought you over here?"

"I had to because I see a very attractive woman here that I'm interested in." "Oh how sweet, I see you not a shy person."

"Of course not, I couldn't just let you walk by and not say anything, so what would you like anything to drink?"

"I would like some baileys with no ice please."

"Alright I'll be right back."

About time I just wanted to get my drink on and start dancing.

"Slimazz, I see you doing you."

"Shayne, this one looks like he got money in the bank."

The night went well until I notice my phone wouldn't stop ringing. So I went outside to tell Richie stop calling me.

"Look boy you need to leave me the fuck alone! I'm serious cause I have no problem getting my cousin on your ass!"

"Which cousin is that, is your cousin's name Blacks?" In the back of my mind I was wondering how he knew my cousin's name.

"Oh, I just wanted to let you know that I like that nice sexy white top you have on."

Now I was getting scared, this motherfucker is watching me. Soon as I start looking around for this crazy nigga, I see Jay coming outside.

"Hey Slim, just checking up on you, are you okay?" Having the phone on my ears I hear Richie telling me I better not say anything to him.

"Oh that's sweet but I'm fine."

"Yes indeed that's what you are." Out of nowhere that's when I've seen Richie walking up towards us.

"Didn't I tell your stubborn ass not to talk to him." I could tell Jay didn't like him, and some problems was about to start.

"Who the fuck is you to tell her who she could talk to?"

"Well motherfucker, this is my woman!"

"No I'm not Richie, so just leave!"

"It's looks like to me she doesn't want you young boy." Then Richie came out of nowhere and gave him the first punch, before you knew it there was a big fight. I hurry up and went inside to get somebody to break it up. By the time I came back outside, there was a big crowd of people being nosey.

"Damn Slimazz, you got niggas fighting over you."

"Look Shayne, Richie been watching me, like he was outside watching me and talking to me at the same time."

"Good thing you leaving soon, just change your number by then he will forget about you."

Finally, the fight stops and I just stayed inside watching the way Richie was so mad like he wanted to kill him. Then he just walks off like nothing happen. I couldn't believe how he was acting like we were together; it was just a one-night stand! See niggas could do it but

when a female has game like them they just go crazy. Guess I really need to give New York a break.

Driving to the airport was just silence, mom was just playing her music acting like she was in the best mood. She wouldn't even try to have a good conversation with me before I leave. So she finally drove up to the airport.

"Phylisia safe trip, and make sure you behave yourself, oh I forgot you have no other choice."

I just took my bags and headed on my way. While walking and thinking to myself; I wonder is it that hard to say I love you? Like she doesn't even know what's going to happen to me, or if she will ever see me again. Me getting love from my mom was just like seeing monkeys jumping off a plane, so impossible.

Finally, I have landed, I was excited to see my dad. I wanted to know if he changes, if he gotten fat, or even taller. Then suddenly I turn around and seen my dad there with a big smile on his face.

"Daddy! I miss you!"

"Hey big girl, how was your flight?"

"Oh, it was okay, I just wanted to hurry up and get off."

"So how everybody back home doing?"

"Everybody doing fine, except for you know who."

"See like or not that's your mother, so keep the peace."

"I know dad that's why I moved here with you, hoping that me and her can get close."

My dad wasn't a money man, but yet still he's our father. Always remember money doesn't buy love which is so true; but of course a lot of people lack happiness because they don 't have money, weird isn't it. Driving to dad's house that's when he chooses to tell me something.

"Look here baby girl I want you to respect my lady, I know it will be hard for you to get use to her but try. Remember she is in my life too."

I was listening to him, but at the same time I was thinking, my dad is really living with a new bitch! We finally reach her house, and all I can say is oh boy.

"Hi Phylisia, I heard a lot about you, my name is Ronda it's nice to finally meet you."

The way she was talking to me I can tell there was something hiding behind that fake smile.

"So I'm going to show you to the room that you will be staying in, and make yourself comfortable."

Remember she told me to make myself comfortable so I went into the living room to watch some TV. I started to smell something good, it's been a long time since I smell some of dad's cooking. I could tell he was happy that I was here because he even gave me a welcome home dinner. Out of nowhere my mom called me.

"So I see you reach safe, how your new life treating you?"

"Well dad is happy that I'm here."

"So did you met your stepmother?"

"Oh yea I met her, but I don't trust her."

"Well you better not start nothing, but if anything goes wrong call me okay.?"

"Alright mom bye, love you."

"Oh love you too, call you later."

See that was the first time we ever had a nice calming conversation, and she sound so concern. Now I know that I came down here for a reason because it's already working.

So we were all sitting at the table eating until Ronda told me to wash up when I'm done.

At first I was thinking, didn't I just came in and she wants me to wash up some damn dishes!

The way I looked at her dad could tell that I didn't like her. While I was washing up dad came up to me and said:

"Look here Phylisia school start over here a month earlier then New York, so next week you start and you may not know it but she is helping you out. So helping out in this house shouldn't be a problem."

Knowing that school starts next week I was kind of excited to see how these country people were. At the same time, I know this lady was going to give me problems.

"Dad lets watch a movie together."

"Alright baby girl I'm coming."

I could tell she didn't like me taking dad away from her like that but shit, she had him for herself for how many years now? So he gave her a kiss and got up from the bed they were laying on and followed me into the living room. I felt really good spending time with dad and

watching a nice movie with him. Until out of nowhere his little bitch came,

"Alright guys I'm going to bed, goodnight."

I thought she was just saying goodnight until dad said,

"Look baby girl it's time for us to go to bed we got a long day tomorrow."

Watching him give me a kiss goodnight then walking to his bedroom, I just thought that's fuck up he could have waited 30 more minutes. That's when I knew I couldn't stand her!

She was just taking my dad away from me after I haven't had him in my life majority of the time. All I know is that wasn't going to happen I was going to get my dad back like it or not.

"Love Comes and Goes"

The sky is blue so why I can't see you?

I miss your kiss and your lovely smile

Your voice that always gives me chills through my spine

I miss your hugs and the night under the sheets

But it's hard to see you cause your always in the streets

My nights are cold, but I wish I could have your soul

I miss the walks through the park, and the stuff we use to talk

Why you had to leave I loved you so much

But then I stop and said to myself:

Love comes and goes, changes is life

Just like the sky isn't always your life.

"Suicide"

School started really quick for me. Over here is so different comparing to New York, like places over here is so far out that I have to take the school bus. The only time I seen a school bus back home is for the disable kids. I finally reach the school and all I can say is wow! This school was so beautiful to the point that they have more than one building. If you have to go to your next class, you have to go outside to the next building. Even at lunch time we can sit outside where the food court is, and eat. Kids over here be living the life to the point where they can drive to school, now this is what you call college life. Coming from a one building school, where everybody right up your ass trust me I can finally say, I love going to school!

See there weren't a lot of black people in North Port High School, so all the black people stuck together. Everybody wanted to know who I was, and where I came from. I know there were a lot of fake people here, that would smile in my face and behind my back they be

talking shit. This is different from back home, because if someone doesn't like you trust me you would know. The only difference that made me uncomfortable was that everybody here was so friendly. They be waving hello to me and they don't even know me. See that shit right there be scaring me, they got me here watching my back and shit.

So I'm here eating my lunch by myself, and here comes the black crew, all I know they better not be here starting any problems.

"Well, well look what we got here fresh meat, hello my name is Alex."

"Okay, hello Alex so what are you going to do with this fresh meat?"

The way he was looking at me I can tell he was feeling this fresh meat, and homeboy wasn't looking too bad his self. Before he could even respond back one of the black girls from the crew decided to jump in.

"Oh, girl don't mind him that's how he is all the time. I can see you not from here, so where you from?"

By the time I look around I have a table full of these kids so interested in me. I figure it wouldn't be hard for me to become popular here.

"Well I just move here from New York."

"Oh, New York! I never been there before, I heard its fast pace over there." Okay the way they were so excited about New York, and the way these girls just talk like white girls is annoying! So the bell rung and I was looking at my schedule wondering which building I have to go to. Then I notice that Alex guy starting walking over.

"It looks like you going to be lost; you want me to help you find your class?" "Oh that's nice but won't you be late to your class?"

"No worries this won't be the first time, so you never told me your name." "Well my name is Phylisia, but for short everybody just calls me Slim."

"I like Phylisia, that's a nice name, you wouldn't mind me call you by your name?"

In the back of my mind I was saying you can call me whatever you like but you know I have to keep my guards up.

"It's nice that you like my name but I just rather you call me Slim."

"Okay! Miss thing, I see you got a New York attitude, but to tell you the truth...I like it. Well here is your class; I guess I see you later?"

"I guess so, thanks."

Sitting down in my class I couldn't get him off my mind, he was just so cute. He had the perfect chocolate skin tone that I just wanted to kiss him all over. It looks like I got a new crush, I just hope this one don't fall in too fast or too deep. School was over, walking over to the school bus I see this loud car driving up towards me.

"Hey Slim, I wouldn't mind dropping you home."

So of course here comes my prince charming.

"How sweet, I see I couldn't get off your mind today."

Walking over to his car I knew he was going to be my little lover boy.

"So do you like it here?"

"The only thing I like over here is the school setting that's all, other than that it's too country for me. I can tell that there's not much for you to do over here."

"Well I throw a lot of house parties, that's what we do most of the time."

"So what do you do at these house parties because I never been to one, all I use to do is go clubbing."

"House parties is simple all we do is bring the music, bring the alcohol, and just do whatever we want."

"Okay, do whatever you want like fucking upstairs in the bathroom?"

"You funny, but yes if that's something they want to do."

"So y'all little bad people behind closed doors."

"That's something I don't do because I don't have a girl I can do that with."

"Well who say you need a girl to do that with, all you can do is just pick up some girl and do your thing then say bye, I enjoyed myself."

"Damn, I'm not cold like that...I like to have one girl that I can do all my shit with, that's just me."

I notice that this guy was different, I mean which guy rather have a girl then just fucking whoever he wants. To tell the truth I really do like his attitude, I can say for once I find a young guy that's mature for his age, which turned me on. Pulling up to the house I know that I wasn't ready for him to leave yet but then again I can't seem too thirsty.

"Well thank you for the ride."

"I would like to talk to you sometimes, so here my number, you can call me at any time."

After hearing those words come out of his mouth that's when I knew he was feeling me.

"Okay, make sure you listen out for my call then."

"I wouldn't miss it for the world, love." Walking to the front door all I can think is; living here wasn't that bad, I felt stress free, no drama but the only problem I have now was I'm starting to miss my mom and my sisters.

Hopping onto the couch I happen to get a call from mom. "So how was your first day of school?" "It was nice, I met a couple of people, including this hot guy."

The way my mom and I been talking I can tell this is what we needed, because now we finally have that nice mother and daughter bound.

"Well as usual, you can't keep them boys off of you."

"Yeah I know, but let's see what happen, I'm going to talk to you later, okay?" "Alright, I'm going to call and check up on you later."

Months went by and mom and I were the best friends ever, but I still wasn't happy. There was something missing, I felt alone even though I had my little boo thing. It was the weekend and I was home with dad, and I decided to talk to him.

"Dad there is something I need to talk to you about."

"Okay, and what is that?"

"Well, mom and I settle our differences so I was thinking to go back home."

"So because you think you're ready to leave you could just get up and go? No I don't think so you got to finish your school year here first."

I couldn't believe the way he was acting; like he need me here.

"Dad, I really don't have to wait until I finish school, I can just leave on the next holiday that's coming up."

"See now I see why you and your mother never gotten along because your ass don't listen!"

Out of nowhere he just picks up one of his speakers to throw at me. I had to hurry up and move before he hit me with that big thing, and that's when I just went to the bathroom. The only thing I can do is cry, and wonder why when I finally got close to mom I just can't get to her. I was tired of crying so I started to look around the bathroom until I found bottles of dad's medications.

I look at myself in the mirror and all I can say to myself is no matter what I do I can never be happy. So what's the sense of me staying alive anymore. For the first time I was giving up on my life, I just didn't care anymore. So I did the unthinkable, I took 17 of his pills while closing my eyes hoping not to open them again. Minutes pass by and right when I notice I was still alive I just started crying all over again, like why god didn't take me? Why am I still alive!

Before I knew it I started feeling weak and dizzy. So I just went to my bed to lay down, while I was laying there I couldn't believe that I just tried to kill myself. Like am I really losing it? It's hard that I did all this moving just for mom and I to be close. Then when my wish finally came true here comes somebody in the way. As you can tell I just hate my life, it's not like I can live my life because the way dad is so strict, then on top of that living in this country ass place. Over here was so damn boring to the point where you don't even see people outside enjoying this hot weather. This place is not for me; this is a place for those old retirements that don't do nothing but lock up in the house. At the same time, I knew I wasn't going to be here long because the way dad just let his temper out on me, I could tell he wouldn't mind me leaving. I was not going to stay around here too long with that temper of his, that shit was just bringing back memories.

When I woke up I could tell I was knock out, I pick up my phone to see the time. Then I saw a miss call from mom, I guess dad spoke to her about me earlier. So I figure to just call her back hopefully I would hear some good news.

"Hey mom I seen you called."

"Yes I did, I heard you got your dad mad over there, are you alright?" Of course she would ask me that question out of anybody she should know about his temper.

"He tried to throw that big old speaker at me on the patio, just because I told him I wanted to go back home to you."

I know that she misses me too so me going back home wouldn't be a problem. "Alright Phylisia, I see that you were doing good but I don't want when you come back home then you back to the old you."

"Alright mom and the same goes for you, I notice you are calmer."

"I'm going to book you a ticket, just don't get on your dad's bad side."

"Thanks mom, bye."

I'm happy that I'm leaving the only problem is I'm going to miss Alex, so I figure to give him a call.

"Hey boo, what's up I was just about to call you."

I could tell that he really does like me, but hey he's young so he will move on quick.

"Well I have some bad news to tell you, I'm going back home."

"Damn, it's like that you just going to get up and leave?"

"I knew you was going to be mad, but baby we could still talk because I'm still coming down to visit."

"You know how I feel about you; you know I love you just promise me you not going to forget about me."

"Alright baby I promise I would keep in touch." The situation I was in I really didn't have time for a relationship anyways.

"LIFE"

Life is a very special thing that I have no choice but to have

Love is life, mistakes are life, and forgiveness are life.

But some people don't get it

Life only comes once, but it won't come again

Time is what you need in life

But some people don't have enough time to achieve what they want

You have to love your life because it only comes to you once and that's a fact!

"Guardian Angel"

My mom didn't care if it was the end of the school year or not, she still brought my ticket to come back home. I felt so much better that I was back home, I couldn't lie but I miss my streets. I can't believe that I actually miss riding the bus and the train, back in the country the only way you could get around is if you have a car. Which sucks, like what if your car breaks down or can't start then your ass is just grass. The only thing that I miss over there would have to be their high class school.

The next day I had an appointment to meet up with my photographer. Modeling is my dream I do believe I have the perfect look to become a successful one. So after school mom came to pick me up because she was my personal stylist. She was quiet excited for me, and I was very excited that she took time out of her busy schedule to come and support me. I took this day very serious, like who knows who would be looking at my photos when I'm done. Or hopefully this damn photographer would hook a sister up and introduce me to some modeling agencies. Barbizon modeling school really did help me out with my walking skills, and my photo shoots, too bad I had to leave to go to Florida. He really did help me out with the comp cards he given me, because after all the hard work we did I had to mail out a lot to modeling agencies.

That day mom finally opens up to me when she finally told me how she wanted to become a model but my dad didn't want her doing that. He told her that her job was to be a mother and to take care of her kids. So I know deep down inside she wouldn't mind me continuing her dream. Days went by smooth for me, I was back in dirty ass Evander

Childs High School, but it wasn't too long till people heard I was back in town. Then that's when I met this skinny guy name Bones, see he had his shit going on. He was a big hustler, with his own car, own crib, all he wanted was a woman by his side he could spoil, in which I wouldn't mind.

So one day I was outside talking to him then that's when mom told me to come inside in which I did, but then she seen him and just got mad.

"You love men too damn much! What you doing outside talking to that grown ass man, do you know what their ass want? All they want is some damn free pussy, and the way you look so damn easy I won't be surprise."

The way her mouth was so loud I had to take a glimpse to see if this guy drove off already because I knew she was trying to embarrass me. I was trying to let her know it wasn't like that but of course she wasn't trying to listen. All of a sudden out of nowhere, she grabs up a hammer and hit me with the back fork of the hammer. Right on my chest blood was just running down, and all I did was gave her a look and ran out of the house.

Running with tears falling from my eyes, and blood running down my chest I just couldn't believe my own mother did this to me. I got on the 5 train didn't know where I was going, didn't know what to do but cry. Like was it that serious for her to pick up a hammer and hit me on my chest, as though she wanted me to just drop down dead. Sitting down and just sobbing with tears just looking down, trying my best not to look up at anybody. Out of nowhere someone came to sit next to me.

"Oh, darling I know it's hard, but I promise you this...you're going to be a real strong person...your time will come."

While sitting down on the train all I can feel is cold shivers. Listening to that lady I had to whip my eyes to see who this woman was because I had some questions to ask her. As soon as a pull my head up there was a cold chill that I felt ran past me, but there was no one sitting next to me. I look around but there wasn't no lady on the train, plus the train didn't stop so no one could have gotten off. Tears started to fall down when I look at my reflection through the train window while looking at the blood just ribbing down from my chest. Was I hearing things, or am I really going crazy for the first time in my life an angel spoke to me. Yeah, yeah at first I never believe that could happen but that night was so cold for me. Like there was someone out there that just gave me love that I didn't even know...someone far from my mom.

"That Girl"

Look at that girl

Why is she crying so much?

No one understands her, no one cares about her

She would cry herself to sleep and wish she could never wake up the next morning

Everybody thinks it's her fault, but what is she doing?

She's innocent!

Will this girl see the good part of her life?

Or will it continue this way?

Are you sorry for that girl or not cause "that girl" is ME!

"Medicine for The Brain"

Days went by, and giving my mom the silence treatment was the only option I had to do. I didn't want to be around nobody, I wasn't even going to school. Thinking about what happen to me all I do is cry myself to sleep. Now that we weren't talking, her favorite daughter was my sister Kelly-Ann.

She was now making sure everything was okay by her, that wouldn't surprise me because I wasn't home most of the time. I tried my best not to be home when I know mom would be there, I just didn't care anymore. I been thinking to myself like when I was living with dad we were close, but when I'm here everything change. I think it's New York, and the only way for this to stop is if we all move.

Waking up every morning now I be feeling weak, weak to the point where I can't pick up my arm. So one-day mom just came in my room and just said: "Hurry up and get ready we going to the doctor, something wrong with you."

When she said that all I can think is, no something wrong with your ass! I just hate going to the damn doctor, the only thing they good for is looking for something wrong with you. Sitting down in the waiting room, after taking a whole lots of tests my doctor came in.

"Phylisia, can I talk to you alone please?"

By the way he said that I knew that it's some bad news he got to tell me.

"Have a sit, now is there anything, or anyone bothering you?"

"No, why?" Of course y'all all know who is, but the doctor doesn't need to know that!

"The reason why I ask is because your stress level is really high for a young girl. I hate to tell you this but you have "Epilepsy".

Hearing that tears just start falling, that sound like I have a big disease and I was about to die.

"What is "Epilepsy?"

"See "Epilepsy" is a mental disorder that effect the brain, some people are born with it but in your case you just got this because of your stress level. Which causes seizures, I know you wondering what is seizures?

Now seizures are when you have episodes that cause you to blank out. Then when you get back to yourself your just weak and can't remember anything that happen. My advice to you is try your best not to stress out so much and believe me or not it can be worst. So from now on you will be on this medicine name "Keppra", you will be on this until you turn 18 then we will see from there. Everything would be alright just make sure you take your medication on time."

I couldn't believe what I was hearing, so basically my mom made me sick! Just when I thought my life couldn't get any worse, this bullshit came along. The medication he gave me was big as fuck, and I didn't give a fuck what he was saying I was not taking it! Weeks went by, and I tried my best to prove I didn't have to take that shit. I started going back to school, helping out in the shop, but then I notice that wasn't helping. We still been arguing, like she doesn't even care what I was going through. I just kept everything to myself, when I wake up weak and my bed is wet from urine on myself that's when I knew I had it worse than before.

I'm just so ashamed and embarrassed of taking medication when I'm only 15 years old. Deep down inside I was hating her, she was always complaining that she stress out but look at the one who is sick because of that shit! Everything I went through, and what I'm going through

right now was just ringing in my ear. I didn't care anymore if I was going to die because of this then it's just meant to be, what would I be missing out on nothing but stress. Laying down in my bed all I can say is: I hope the heavens above is listening...why me!

"Why Me"

Why me, I don't deserve this

Why can't the people I care for care me back and most of all why can't we all get along?

My life is cold, lonely, and boring am I the only one who see that?

Time, Time again I ask myself will this change? What will I become of myself?

Sometime I sit back and ask God what does he have plan out for me but he never answer me

back

Does he know what's going on in my life?

Does he know the pain I'm feeling?

I guess not cause if he did he would have helped me

So who do I have to turn to?

A matter of fact I won't stop to turn. I'll just keep on running.

"Welcome Mystery Man To The Family"

I really took my bad news serious, to a point where I had to talk to mom.

"Mom, you may not care but I'm going through a lot."

"You, going through a lot that's funny, after you the one that don't have bills to pay and four kids you have to take care of on your own!"

See the way she thinks after I'm the one that just heard some bad ass news like taking some damn medication! I rather have some little ass bill problem that can go away, and kids so I won't feel alone but as usual she can't appreciate what she has. "Okay mom, since we both are going through some things I think it would be a good idea if we move out of state."

"So you expect me to just give up on my shop just to sacrifice your needs? Well you must be out of your damn mind!"

"Can't you see nothing better is happening over here for us, if you have any love in your heart for me would you just give it a try please?"

By the way she looks at me I could tell she was going to think about it. The only place I could think of that we would know somebody would have to be Georgia. Then I notice something was changing about my mom, but I couldn't put my finger on it. She was smiling more, she wasn't cursing me out, or making a big thing out of nothing as much.

My mom cousin was keeping a barbecue and we were invited. There was a lot of guys there, but I was paying attention to this guy that mom been talking to for over 30 minutes, in which she didn't curse out yet. It was hard to believe it but she looks very happy, my sisters and I was just watching them for the whole night. Maybe this is what she needed was a man by her side, I just hope this work out. Mom would sleep out and come home late like nothing was going on, but who was she trying to fool remember I played the same game before.

Months went by and she finally introduce us to this mystery man his name was "Phillip". I can't lie but I could tell he was a good man by the way he made sure she was okay, and by the way he makes sure we all ate something before we go to bed.

See mom is just a hard woman to please so all the things he was trying to do really didn't matter. Of course relationships can't be peachy perfect all the time. So every time they argue she would come home and just find something to curse me out for as usual. I couldn't take it no more so I told her I was going to take my idea and move to Georgia, because I need to make my life better. Phillip was cool with the kids and I so I called and told him I think it's a good idea for us to move to be a better family. He didn't feel comfortable with me going over there by myself which was weird cause my mom wouldn't give a damn. He finally talks to mom and told her that it wasn't a bad idea, and that's something that we all need. She said I could go and she would come later on with the kids, that's when he told her that he didn't want me to be alone. In my eyes I thought that was so sweet, and mom finally got the family man she needed. I was excited to give this a try,

I felt this was all we needed to have that mother and daughter bound, which was a new location.

Riding on the bus to Georgia with Phillip, I could tell he was happy to start a family with mom. We finally reach Lawrenceville, GA where we had to book a hotel room. We had two twin bed, deep down inside I did feel a little weird because he was really friendly.

"Phylisia do you want to lay down next to me, and watch a movie with me?" "Oh, no thanks I'm fine here in my bed".

Now what the fuck was that about! Please don't tell me he was just flirting with me, or maybe I was just overreacting. Before I jump to any conclusions let me just see what this man is really about.

"It's Him"

Who's the one that wake you up every morning?

Who's the one that make sure your safe and warm, and would never give up on you?

I hope you know who I'm talking about

He's the one you can trust with no secret aside

He also knows everything about you, and know what's right for you to what's wrong

He's the one that show love like no one else can

I'm going to leave it up to you, I have a feeling you know who it is

It's Him!

"Education is the Key"

It didn't take me long to start school, I notice Georgia system was really slow comparing to New York. The school wasn't nice like in Florida, but of course much better then in New York. It didn't take me long to fit in, but I can tell they was real racist in Gwinnett county.

Over here they go by counties cause it's so huge and space out, the only way you can go somewhere is by driving. I'm not going to lie but this shit was driving me crazy! I mean they don't even have a damn corner store you can just walk to.

Time went by fast, mom and the kids eventually came down and we moved into this nice big house. See once your use to New York style of houses and move down in the south everything is bigger for cheaper. My sixteen birthday came and all we did was cut a little cake at the house and that was it, so I didn't have a sweet sixteen which sucks. The only good part was my boyfriend from back home was coming to live with us. I know what you thinking, like my mom really approve of that? Yes, she did! Of course I had to beg her but she said as long my grades stay good then it wouldn't be a problem. I met Joe when I moved back home from Florida. He was a Jamaican DJ who happen to hear about me being such a heartbreaker, so he figured the reason why is because I never met him before. So you can say he was ready for a challenge no matter what it took, even moving to another state to be with me.

Everything these past couple of months was just fine. Mom got a nice job, and Phillip was like a stay at home dad making sure our belly was full every night. Phillip was a seventh day Adventist, so he found a Jamaican church and just like that mom and the kids start going there. I did feel a way because I'm use to my Sunday church and all of a sudden this man came and just started changing things. I can tell that they like this church because it was a way they can make friends, including mom like what would she do without people? It didn't take long for her to start doing hair again, she got people from in the church and forward on.

She starts doing it in the house and of course I had to help the only good thing is now I get a little side money from helping her. See this is all I wanted was for my mom to have a clear mind which will make us all happy. Now she got a man by her side, even though he is never working like how she is but still she should be grateful she got a helper. As usually I started getting nervous and saying to myself this was too easy, I just had a feeling something bad was going to happen. As you can tell by now reading this book good luck doesn't follow me to well. Waking up the next morning getting ready to go to school I felt really good, and hoping they would do me the honor and skip my grade with their slow asses.

"Phylisia don't forget to take your medication."

"Okay mom I got to go before I miss the bus."

See mom make sure she reminds me to take them because it's hard to remember to take something you're not use to. I had to hurry up to my first period class because his old ass would close the door a minute after you supposed to be in, then you have to get a late pass. So I made sure I was on time so this man wouldn't have an excuse not to like me.

"Excuse me, but can I please use the bathroom?"

"Yes you may."

Soon when I was finish and about to go back to class I remember the pill I have to take. It wouldn't make no sense if I go in the class to come back out so let me just go to my locker and get my pill then go in. When I was walking back to the classroom I seen him standing outside waiting on me.

"Well, well I see you been A-hall walking."

"What is A-hall walking I just had to go to my locker after I went to the bathroom that's all."

"Oh, save it for the principle I'm going to tell her you been walking around in the hallway when you supposed to be in class."

Now tell me this motherfucker is not racist! So he brought me in the principle office by the way she looks at me I can tell she just another racist bitch!

"So your teacher told me you been A-hall walking, so you have 5 days' suspension."

"So you going to suspend me for a week just because of what this teacher said? Don't you know that there's always two sides of a story? So whatever he says it's right? Now that's some bullshit!"

Of course I was piss the fuck off! See I never had gotten suspended before, the way I was so upset I wanted to knock her out so instead I just walk out of her office. While walking to go outside I see cops coming towards me.

"Madam you have to go outside."

"Okay that's where I was going."

Walking outside I didn't know this would be a big deal for her to call some damn cops on me.

"Now you can tell me what happen."

Telling him what happen I can tell it didn't make a difference because as usually its whatever they say is what goes.

"Well she doesn't want you on school property anymore so call someone to pick you up."

"That little ass problem and now she doesn't want me back in school and just like that she fucks up my education!"

"Madam calm down because I can lock you up."

How can these people be so heartless, so cold like was it this serious for her to mess up my education? Having Phillip pick me up I knew it was going to be some problems with mom tonight. When I reach home all I could do is go in my room and cry, and I really didn't want to hear from nobody. My boyfriend "Joe" came in and just hold me tight in his arms, which was so sweet but that was something I was just getting used to.

"Baby I heard what happen and them kicking you out of school just because you had a to go your locker is some bullshit, the only person that can try to work this out is your mom."

Out of nowhere I hear mom's mouth coming from upstairs cursing my ass out.

"This is your damn problem! You can never just shut the fuck up, instead you have to run off your damn mouth every fucking time which put you in deeper problem!"

"So I don't have a right to let her know what she was doing was wrong, like who in the fuck doesn't know there is two sides of a story? What if the man wanted to rape me off or something? I don't give a fuck, that school need to be sued because if the teachers can just lie on students for no reason that's bullshit!"

"See you don't have no damn respect for me that's why bad luck going to follow your ass. You lucky, you got yourself into this problem you can find yourself out of it, remember you grown now."

The way I spoke to her I know I was wrong but she should understand I was upset, like who wouldn't be? I knew she wouldn't care, and wouldn't do anything about it. If you didn't want to hear my opinion I think that was real cold, because if one of my child got kick out of school and she didn't do anything major wrong like; fighting in school, or bring a weapon into school then I would take it serious. I can't lie now I was missing New York more, because back home you can't get kick out just because you have a mouth.

A good week went by until I got a letter in the mail, it was telling me the school I have to attend now is called the "The Give Center". Now this school sound like a special school, do they seriously think that I'm crazy? Mom read the letter and told me it looks like this is a school for bad kids, like yourself. This was weird that Georgia actually have different schools for bad kids.

"Well Phylisia you start Monday, and you have to wear uniform no bus picks you up in this school good thing it's near by the house so you can walk from school".

When Monday finally came and entering the school I notice they have metal detectors at the doors, just like back home. So I was real curious for what was the reason they need all of that in this country ass place. The classrooms were real small plus the students and I looked alike which drove me crazy!

I notice that the students in here were slower, the teachers were acting like they were teaching some damn middle school students. So I had a white lady teacher for math, and by the way she teaches I can tell she doesn't have much patience I can tell she was problem. There was this girl that sat next to me she was cool but her weakness was algebra, which was my favorite so I figure to help her.

"Excuse me Ms. Phylisia, what are you doing?"

"Oh nothing really I was just showing her an easier way so she can remember the work."

"So your taking over my job now? May I ask why she couldn't just ask me?" "Maybe because she was scared to ask you, I don't know but you can ask her."

By the way she was looking at me I could tell she wanted to curse me out, but again was it that serious?

"Ms. Phylisia follow me outside please."

Walking outside I knew what was about to happen again, and I just didn't care anymore.

"I didn't like the way you spoke to me in front of those students."

"Okay I understand I was just trying to help someone, if she couldn't understand it your way then there's another way she can learn it."

"Well I just don't feel comfortable with you in my class anymore so I will report this, so let's go to the principal's office."

Sitting in the office while they were outside talking I had so much anger inside and I was going to tell this woman how I feel if they kick me out again.

"Well, Ms. Phylisia your teacher just told me what happen and once a teacher report

a student in this Give Center you are out, sorry we don't give these students any chances in

here because they shouldn't be here in the first place."

"So what's going to happen from now on?"

"You can go get your G.E.D that's your only way I see it for you."

"So that's it! You kick me out of school just because I was helping out a damn

student?

It's not my fucking fault that you have some dumb ass teachers that work here which looks like they can't even get their damn masters!"

Walking out the school I just didn't give a fuck who feelings I hurt all I know was that they were not going to stop my education just like that.

"Where's My Hero"

Feeling so alone, so cold

Can't stop the tears from falling down your face

Wondering what to do next

Having no one by your side, no one to talk to

Always have to work extra hard never been that lucky

But do I really have a hero?

To help guide me to the right way

To show me all these pain would one day go away

Does this hero even know my name

Knows what to do to cure my pain

All I really what to know is do I really have a hero?

"LOVE IS PAIN"

A good two months went by and I was still home not doing anything. Deep down inside anger was building up so bad to the point where old Slim was coming out. Joe was getting on my nerves, well to tell the truth I'm so embarrassed of him. When I met him back home he told me he was 22 years old and just the other day he told me he was 17. Of course I was mad because I love my older guys but I didn't take that serious unlike his height. Just because of his height I didn't feel comfortable going out with him, face it I never been with a guy shorter than me. Well it didn't matter to my family because they love him like he was part of the family already. To be honest I didn't care anymore, the only thing I wanted to do is party and have fun. So late in the night I would have niggas pick me up, then have any other nigga I can get to drop me off back home. Walking to the door one night I had a feeling Joe would be up waiting on me, so I tried my best to sneak in.

"Wow! Look at the time you choose to come in 5'o clock in the damn morning!"

"What are you doing staying up for me? You could at least go to bed no one is stopping you."

"You want me to just go to bed when you have different, different man dem pick you up and drop you off! So you fucking around?"

The way he was cursing me out I knew I wasn't ready for no damn man staying up and watching my every move. Shit he couldn't please me anyways, the only thing he was good at was making sure everybody else was happy.

"Look Joe I don't have time to argue with you tonight so I see you when I get up."

I can't lie I was drunk and listening to him would give me a damn headache. When I got up I notice he was giving me the silence treatment, he would just walk pass me like he doesn't know me. Well I didn't care, if he wanted to act like that I will let him be and do me.

Everybody left to go to church so I figure to go play some music and just start working out.

"Phylisia I know you fucking around on me! You be coming home early in the damn morning, then when I do call you don't answer your damn phone!"

"Joe, just leave me alone because I don't have a reason to go and sleep around."

Out of nowhere he grabs my arm and said: "Don't think I would let you disrespect me, so you better know who you fucking with!"

"Get off of me! Do you really think I'm scared of your short ass!"

Before I could even finish cursing him out he just gave me a big ass punch in my face.

Which I fell to the ground trying my best to fight for my life I tried to get up but all I could feel is him kicking the shit out of me and yelling at the top of his lungs.

"Yeah you take man for fool! Now you know not to fuck with me!"

I finally got near to the phone where all I could do is dial 911 before he notices what I was doing.

"You little bitch! You going call cops on me knowing my situation!"

See he didn't have any papers so basically he could get deported back home to Jamaica. When he notices what I did he just start beating on me even worse and trust me I did try to fight back until I had a chance to run outside. I can't lie for a little short nigga he was real strong, finally the cops came right of the middle of him trying to drag me back in the house.

"Sir, put your hands up where I can see them."

He did everything the cop told him to do, which surprise me I thought he would try to run off. While the cop handcuff him, he asked me some questions:

"Okay by all the bruises on your face I can tell he was fighting you. So how long have this been going on?"

"Well this is the first time we ever been in a fight."

"Now can you tell me his name please."

As soon he asked me that question I just happen to look at Joe with tears running down his eyes, and I just felt sorry for him. It was like I didn't even remember what he just done to me I just didn't want him to get deported all because of me.

"His name is "Rick Davis."

Where I got that name from I don't know, but all I know is he won't get deported with a fake name but he needed to learn his damn lesson if he thinks it's okay to hit me again.

Watching them drove away all I could do is cry, I still couldn't believe he did this to me, now I know what they mean when they say love can hurt. I had letters come in the mail for me every week from Joe. Reading them I can tell that he hates it there and he learned his lesson. I just couldn't forgive him, so I made sure I never wrote him back or went to visit him. Since I been home all alone when the kids went to school I would just stay in my bed and talk to my friend that I met back home in New York. His name was "Will", this guy I met when I was back home in NY walking with Shayne going shopping. I wasn't talking to mom either, a good three months went by and she still haven't done anything with me and school. Talking on the phone with Will I just needed a friend to talk to.

"I'm so tired of just staying in this damn house every day, and this lady don't even give a fuck about how I feel as usual."

"Well, if you're brave enough you can come stay with me over here."

At first I thought to myself, how long do I know this guy again, but the amount of anger I have built up in me I just didn't give a fuck no more.

"Are you serious, because I would start packing my shit right now."

"Yes I'm serious I would pay for your bus ticket for this weekend, and you better come because I do want to see you."

"So I guess this is the plan, I will see you this weekend, thanks boo."

Getting off the phone I started packing, if you think about it what's the sense of me staying here might as well I go back home anyways. I was real excited to go back home so I had to call up Shayne and let her know that I was coming.

"Guess what girl! I got a surprise for you!"

"What is it you know I hate to guess."

"Okay, anyways remember your little friend we met on Fordham

Rd?"

"Yea, what about him? Do y'all still talk?"

"Yea we been talking for like a month now since Joe got lock up."

"Damn Slim you just wrong."

"Anyways, mom not doing anything about my school situation so my new boo is going to buy my ticket to come over there this weekend!"

"Okay that's what's up, so I can start letting people know who's coming back." "Now be careful who you tell because I really don't need no drama, okay."

While I was getting ready for this weekend I decided to tell mom where I'm going instead of just running away, remember what she said "I'm grown."

"Mom, since nothing is happening over here for me I decided to go back home."

"And who you going to stay with?"

"I'm going to be staying with my friend "Will" he said it would be fine, I just need to try to get my life together."

"Well, I understand because you don't have anything over here to loose, but I need you to be careful."

As you can tell my mom don't cause a big scene when I want to leave to go somewhere, which I didn't understood I'm just 16. Maybe she was just so use of me leaving and coming right back home with her. I was so happy that she didn't make it a big deal, but I think deep down inside she just doesn't have time to help me right now. See she's the only one working, and paying the bills plus she got four other kids to support including her husband's son, yes they got married.

My mom husband, Phillip would try to get jobs but in Gwinnett county that's not a walk in the park. This place is for those medium class people, with careers the most thing I hate is that you need a damn car to go anywhere. The weekend came and my ticket was waiting on me at the Greyhound bus station, so Phillip decided to dropped me off.

Mom was busy sleeping from her crazy night job. I don't know why I was thinking I was going to get any goodbye love, yea that was something only the crackers do I guess.

Riding on the bus it was long and exhausted, but I still couldn't wait to be back home. I couldn't believe I was going to try a future with this man, and hopefully everything would add up. Thinking to myself I had to think negative, like what if my age mess me up from working towards my future. Deep down inside I have to keep my hopes up, what do I have to lose? Nothing, all I can do is give it a try.

"Look"

Look at the sky isn't it always blue?

Look at the stars isn't it always bright?

Look at the kids isn't it a good sight?

You should always look up before you look down and that's not lie

Look at the fishes in the sea

It's good to look but you should always listen too

Listen to the birds chirping

Listen to the breeze blowing

Listen to the joy of laughter

See it's good to look and it's good to listen, that's why you could do both

"Sex to Reality"

When I reach back home I felt so relax, hoping something good will happen. I was on a mission to go back to school and try to get my life together. Living with Will was like we were running away slaves. We move to three different apartments, and he would never explain to me why. Days were going slow for me, and no matter what I try to do I still felt alone. Shayne and I weren't going out often because she had school to go to. I did try to go back to school but of course I needed a parent with me. Thinking to myself I do have family here but why is it so hard for them to try to help me? Yes, they do have their own problems and life to live, but helping out family shouldn't be such a crime. I tried my best to block everything out so I decided to try to make dinner for the first time instead of the regular microwave food.

"Will, I need you to go to the store for me and get some stuff so I can try to make something to eat."

"Oh man! Do you really expect me to go outside to buy some food that you can just experiment on?"

"Your rude ass should be fucking happy I'm over here about to make food for your dumb ass! You just so fucking ungrateful I can tell you haven't had a real woman before; fuck it you don't have to worry about me trying to do anything good for you again!"

I was real heated like that nigga should be lucking I wanted to fucking cook, and that's something I don't do. So I just went in the kitchen to make the regular noodles soup to eat not saying a word to that jackass. I been staying with him for a good two weeks and it would be the same thing over and over again. We would always argue then in the next couple of

minutes we are back to normal.

"Baby I have my boys coming over just to chill soon."

His friends came by and I just stayed in the room until I was bored and I wanted to see what they were up to. This was the first time I have met his homeboys the only funny part was that they were all white.

"Okay you know I have to introduce you guys to my girl right here, isn't she beautiful?"

The way he introduces me to his boys I just figure to chill with them for a little to see what they were up to. Then that's when I notice they was passing a bloat around to smoke in which that is something I don't do but was always a little curious.

"Here babe try this with me it's just a little weed nothing major."

I took it because I knew they was all watching me and took two good pulls like I smoke before. Sitting on his lap I started feeling so seductive, so horny, I just wanted some of him right now.

"Okay boys it was nice chilling with you all but we about to go to bed right now."

"Oh yeah we know what she wants right now."

That was weird, I can't believe I just kick out his friends just because I wanted some dick and I couldn't wait any longer.

"Now that's what I'm talking about, babe do you know we would make a pretty baby."

That's when I just stop and thought to myself why is he thinking about a baby right now and we just met.

"Okay Will you don't have to be thinking about that right now."

"I know I just had to tell you what I was thinking, because I know our baby will be the most beautiful baby we are already the cutest couple."

Listening to him was something I wasn't trying to do for too long since now I know where his mind is at.

"Will, make sure you put on a condom please."

I made sure he put that on right in front of me because no he wasn't going to get a baby by me. He turns the lights off, then we went straight to the business. This was the first time we had sex since I been here, I have waited long enough. The way his skin was nice and soft, black and beautiful you just had to love it. The way he crawls his fingers up my legs passing my knee to my thighs, while he swirls his tongue around my neck making me just want to moan his name out loud. Having me soak and wet just can't wait to feel his dick inside of me.

Listening to him calling me his baby while he puts on the condom and turn off the light. Finally feeling so release that I can feel his nice wide, thick dick inside of me.

"Oh baby you like that? This is my pussy right?"

"Oh yes it's all yours, come with it daddy"

"Alright turn around". Having him slap my ass just bought even more pleasure, I couldn't help but to want more.

"Oh baby you feel so damn good! Your pussy is so nice and wet! Oh, Oh, Oh......YES!!!! Baby I just cum inside of you, you going have my baby".

"What! Get the fuck off of me! "Hearing those words come out his mouth I just had to run to the bathroom and try to piss it out. I tried over and over again to pee but it won't come out, so the next step was to go to fuck his ass up! I picked up a frying pan and wanted to beat his ass with it.

"How the fuck you just going to cum inside of me like it's fucking nothing! You think it's a fucking joke, no this is something serious!"

"I know baby but just think about it we going to have a pretty baby though."

Like what the fuck is wrong with this nigga? He not even thinking about the future with this baby, he just worries about how pretty a damn baby is going to be. I had to run out to try to get that morning after pill because I really don't need that sick motherfucker's baby. Walking into Rite Aid I knew they should have it because I remember them selling it here.

"Excuse me where can I find that morning after pill?"

"Well now they change the law that you have to get it prescribe from a doctor now, sorry."

Like what the fuck! Now tell me how am I going to get a doctor over here with no damn insurance, I didn't know what to do but to call mom.

"Mom, I have some news to tell you, something is wrong with Will we just had sex and he just cum inside of me like it's nothing. All he can say is that we going to have such a pretty baby, then on top of everything Rite Aid don't sell the morning after pill like they used to. Now they say that I have to get it prescribe from a doctor, I just don't know what to do."

"Well, it was your idea to move over there with that sick man, but I'm just going to buy you a bus ticket for tomorrow so go get ready."

The way mom was so calm I couldn't believe it, like I was mad and she was acting like oh well something was going to happen sooner or later. I didn't want to go to that nigga's

house because I knew my mind wasn't right and I didn't know what I would do. So I just sat on the curb on White Plains Rd and cry my eyes out, like why me I don't deserve all of this. I knew people that was walking by was looking at me like I was crazy but I didn't care. I just was praying over and over again please don't let me have this baby it would just mess up my modeling, plus I'm not ready, I'm not stable. Leaving his place, I didn't have a word to say to him, I didn't even what to see his face never again.

"That Stranger"

Oh look at him

Does he even remember my name?

Know what I like to eat in the morning or before I go to bed

What's my favorite color to wear or the type of music I love to hear?

All of this would just bring a tear to my eye...but no look at him

I was just his lucky penny he found in his jeans pocket

That he just had to pick it up and throw away

Not caring if he would have needed it one day

I thought they said what goes around comes around

But oh no look at him!

"Surprises Meant for a Lifetime"

Riding on the bus back to Georgia I just found it hard to believe. I went back home to try to start my life over again, and go back to school but as usual nothing happens my way. I just hope and pray to god that I'm not pregnant. A good two months went by and I still haven't seen my period. That's when I see mom walking through my door.

"Phylisia, I know you don't want to believe me but your pregnant you have to go to the doctor."

Of course mom should know she's a nurse plus have four kids so she'd the expert. So I ended up at the clinic, where everybody is so friendly and cheerful. Sitting in the room waiting on my results I just couldn't stop shaking.

"Please god I'm sorry for everything I promise I'll be a good girl, and treat mom better just please don't let me be pregnant".

I know that was odd but what else can I do but pray right now hoping for a miracle to come.

"Well, Ms. Reynolds congratulations! Your eight weeks pregnant!"

Looking at her face with a big smile on it and hearing eight weeks' pregnant echo in my ears, I couldn't help but to cry. I know she felt sorry for me by the way she sat next to me and gave me a hug.

"You know if this is too much for you to handle you can have an abortion done before you reach three months."

When I heard that I had to cry even more because that's something I really didn't believe in. She gave me the final date to come in, if I change my mind or anything. Walking out I can tell everyone knew or had an idea, I just couldn't stop crying. I felt so betrayed how can he be so cold to me like what did I do that was so wrong? A grown ass man like him just treat me like a joke! Like who in their right mind would just have a baby with someone just because their pretty, or sexy, or cute, or even handsome! That's some bullshit! The most fucked up shit was that I don't even know him, two weeks is not enough. Walking to the car mom was sitting there just waiting to hear she was right by looking at my bloody red eyes.

"Well, Phylisia this is probably what you need so you can settle down."

I had so much anger inside of me but most of all, there was pain. What kind of advice was that? Looking at her so calm, like this is nothing, this is what she wanted so I can be such a good girl…that's bull! She's bull! When I got home I just ran inside the room to cry my eyes out. Until I heard a big celebration downstairs with the kids. They ran in my room and said…

"Phylisia, Phylisia, Joe is home!"

Oh damn now tell me bad luck doesn't follow me. Out of all the other days they choose today to discharge him. Deep down inside I just wanted to ran away again but where will I be running to because I still will be pregnant. I didn't want to see him, truthfully I was scared I didn't want another beat down so all I could do is hurry up and lock the door and cry out my pain.

"Phylisia, baby I know you in there because the girls already told me you were." Isn't it funny when your family loves your mate like their part of the family, they so quick to sell your ass out. Knowing him he will keep on knocking on the door until he loses his temper and you know I can't handle that right now so I had to open the door.

"Oh, baby I miss you so much, I'm sorry about everything I did to you so here's a flower I pick for you while I was walking over here. I know how much you love the nice white one's so I made sure I pick this one up just hoping I can see that beautiful smile of yours."

Everything he was saying was so sweet, but me knowing I'm hiding something so big that will change my life forever all I can do is start crying again. I know I had to tell him even if this will break us apart.

"Baby, baby calm down why you crying like this?"

"Joe I have something to tell you."

"Okay what is it? You need to hurry up and tell me because I'm getting worried now."

"Well I went to the doctor earlier today and found out I'm pregnant."

"What seriously! We having a baby, oh I love you."

Obviously he's thinking I'm pregnant by him, should I let this be an episode on Maury; shit the only problem is I can't lie for that long. I really don't know how those girls do it but knowing the person I am I couldn't mislead a person like this specially not this way.

"Well not exactly; see when you were lock up I ended up getting kick out of school so I got mad at mom because she wasn't doing anything about that so I ended up moving back home with this guy. Basically he's the one that got me knocked up because I'm only eight weeks pregnant."

When all was said and done I tried my best not to be too close to him.

"I'm so sorry, I didn't plan this he just did this as a joke or something. I wish I wasn't pregnant but if I had to choose then of course it would have been by you. I'm so sorry I really wish I could turn back the hands of time."

Looking in his eyes I knew he was shock, and I was hoping deep down inside he sees how sorry I am. Most of all I was praying that he wouldn't lose his temper and start beating the shit out of me. I know what happen was fuck up but again I didn't plan for this shit to happen! The way he holds tight I can tell he was crying too. I can 't lie I felt so stupid, guilty, and most of all hopeless. If he was going to leave me I would truly understand.

"Alright let me tell you something from now on this baby is ours, and this is our secret so don't let anyone know what really happened."

When he said those words, I just couldn't believe he would do that for me. I can't lie from then that's when I realize how much I really do love him; I mean wouldn't you?

"Love Is You"

Who is the one?

Who's the one that showed me what love means?

Love is you

Who's the one that stayed by me, knowing what I was doing was wrong

Love is you

Who's the one that tried his best to show me how much my love means to him

Love is you

Knowing that I made a mistake but instead you gave him double the love

Love is you

All those pains we went through, which only made us stronger

Made me realize that's love, I been through love, I had love because

Love is you!

"What's Love?"

Wow I can't lie I was living the life right now! I had my own place, my own car, finally working as an CNA, and most of all I had my own family. I gave birth to Kamari on Aug, 1, 2007 and on that same day that's when Joel propose to me. Everybody was happy, and for the first time I can tell mom was really proud of me. We were all planning the wedding together but then I felt worried like this was too good to be true. I was getting scared I had a strong feeling something was going to happen, knowing me nothing good ever happens for too long. It's going on three months and Joe and I been going on strong with no fights. The way I was so relief and happy that he changed I had to go out and get a drink.

"Alright baby I'm going to go out with some friends I'll be back later."

"Okay so where you going, and why can't I come?"

"Well we don't have no one to watch Kamari right now, and I just need some girls time so please just stay home with our son."

Looking at him I knew he was mad but right now I couldn't let that bother me too much, put it like this it's been too long he had me locked up in the house. Walking into this bar lounge with Ashley I can tell that we had a lot of catching up to do.

"Girl I can't believe you about to settle down with that crazy ass boy of yours, like my home girl used to say: once a man put their hands on you they will always keep doing it. But what do I know girl, I just wish you two good luck though."

By the way she was acting I can tell she already had too much to drink, I couldn't even say anything back because I didn't know if she would be telling the truth. "Excuse me can I get another round."

Shit all I can do is get me another drink and just try to forget what she just told me.

Meanwhile Joe was just calling off my phone like something was wrong I had to rush to the bathroom.

"What happen?"

"Oh so that's how you answer your phone when you out with man."

"No I just thought something was wrong that's all."

"Well I want you to come home now!"

"Look please don't start no argument but I will be home soon okay, bye I love you."

Now what the fuck is his problem, he just going to call off my phone just to tell me to come home! All I can do was think about what home girl said, I guess I would find that out when I get home then.

"Alright girl thanks for taking me out call you later."

Walking to the door I was so scared hoping he fell asleep. Soon as I walked in and turn on the living room light he was there sitting in the dark the whole time waiting for me.

"Oh hey baby I see you up."

"Do you know what time it is? I called you 2:00 in the damn morning to come home, but you choose to come home after 3:00!"

"Alright baby calm down don't wake up Kamari, it's not that serious let's just go to bed."

While I was walking to the room he grabs me and threw me on the couch and started punching the shit out of me.

"Who the fuck you think you talking to like that! You so fucking hard headed! I'm going to kill your stubborn ass!"

"Please stop! Please baby I love you don't do this to me again."

"That's why your dumb ass shouldn't gone out nowhere."

I finally gave him a nice big ass kick and ran to the kitchen and grab a frying pan that was the closest thing that was near me. With all of the loud noise that's when my roommate came out.

"Hey what's going on?"

The way Joe gave him the look I can tell he wanted him back in his room. "Look here man if you don't want to get fuck up you better take your ass back in your room and mind your damn business!"

"Alright man I don't have anything to do with this."

What! I can't believe that tall ass man is just going to listen to this short little ass boy like he's scared of him. That's when I figured to make sure I let my roommate know not to walk away and this shit is serious.

"No, no please call 911 he said he was going to kill me!"

"Wow you think I'm scared of a frying pan?"

While he was walking closer I was trying to find a sharp knife but couldn't find any. So I had no choice but to do some Madea style and hit him on his head with the pan. Finally, I heard the cops at the door.

"I need someone to open this door or we have no choice but to break it down." "Okay so the cops are here to lock my ass up again, but no they won't catch me."

He opens the door to the balcony and jump down and made a run for it. I hurry up to open the door for the cops but by the time they went outside looking for him he was nowhere in sight. I told the cops his real name this time and that he's a Jamaican with no green card.

Looking at myself in the mirror with a black eye, busted lip, and bruises all over my body all I can say is "I guess she was right". Now I have reach a point in my life when I can say "Fuck love!"

I finally can relate to Tina Turner and most of all my mom. Remember I was the one always seeing my dad beating on my mom and now look who it passed on to. When you experience something like this I can really say that it hurts. It's not like you can work it out because that's just him. So of course I have to just let go of love, but I will always love him it's just that I can never be with him again. The only person that knew me, that stood by my side no matter how many downfalls we had. Is now gone, gone out of my life all because of one problem he had. I have to keep my head up high I can't forgive him anymore, because I made a promise that my son would never see a man beat on me no matter how deep my love is.

"My Friend"

She's in love, her heart is hurting, her soul is aching

Maybe she's confuse, does she know what she's doing?

She's in pain, love is pain, life is pain

She doesn't deserve this, she's a nice person

Can I help? Can I help cure her pain?

But to tell you the truth I can't

I hope the pain stop, so she could see the good part of her life

I would hate to tell you this: But sometimes you have to ride the rough road before you ever

reach the smooth!

"The Eye That Bleeds"

After all, that drama, I decided to stay by mom for a while. Just in case he would come back at my place acting like he owns this shit. Even though he knows where my mom lives but at least over here I have more support.

"Oh gosh Phylisia! Look at your face you know you can't go to work like that, you better tell them you sick or something."

"Yeah I know; by the way the supervisor doesn't like me I probably don't have a job to go back to."

"Don't worry, so tell me what happen."

"Well, Joe and I happen to have another fight just because I went out with my home girl."

"So you back partying! After you know he doesn't like you doing that, neither do I!"

See I should of knew not to tell mom anything because as usual no matter how hurt I was it was always my fault.

"That's all you have to say! Why can't you be a nice, loving mother and just hold me? Out of anyone I thought you would understand more because you went through the same shit with dad! So you have no right defending that piece of shit boy that put his hands on me!"

The way I was so upset I had to hurry up and walk away from her before I say or did something stupid. The amount of years my mom putted up with that abuse, and now when I look at it I was the one it passed on to. Yes, I did forgive him a couple of times but hearing those painful words" I'm going to kill you" by someone you love it's like he just stabs and rip out my heart. I know I would never love someone like the way I loved him, but fuck it who really needs love they just want it and for me I don't want anything to do with it. It took a good week for my eye to heal so I figure to call back my job and tell them I'm feeling much better.

"Hello this is Phylisia I'm calling to let you know that I can start back work soon as possible."

"Well I'm glad you feeling better but you coming back won't be necessary."

"Why is that I did call to let you know I was sick."

"Yes, yes I know but one thing about our policy you have to let us know a good 24 hours before your shift that you can't come in. I'm sorry but I wish you luck."

Fuck! What kind of bullshit ass policy is that? Like who can look in a crystal ball and can tell "oh I'm going to be sick tomorrow, so let me tell them." I knew the bitch didn't like me she was looking for an excuse and there she got it. Just when I thought my day couldn't get any worse my phone rang from Joe's number.

"What do you want?"

"Well hello there I'm just calling you to let you know that I got your man now, so don't think about calling back this number bitch!"

"Bitch you can have that little ass boy I hope he beat on your ass next!"

What kind of shit is that? Like who would call any girl up starting some beef for some damn guy? I knew something was different with these bitches over here in the south, because everybody knows up north girls don't have time for that. Guess Joe had no problem moving on because he already have a girl in process. I was real piss off so I decided to go to the barbershop where mom was doing hair at and help her out, since I don't have a job no more.

Walking in the shop guess who I seen sitting in my mom's chair getting their hair done. I couldn't believe it, after we just had a fight my mom has the nerves to do his hair, and I know his ass isn't paying. He just sitting there like he's the man, but how he got over here in the first place?

So I went outside to see if his stupid ass girl brought him here. There she goes, she was sitting in her car talking on the phone waiting for him. I figured it was her because she was the only female in a car waiting on someone. So I had to go over there and let her know who she was talking to and she isn't running shit.

"Hey girl you remember me?"

"Hold on girl, somebody at my window talking to me…no, who are you?"

"Oh wow I see you don't get that loud ass mouth anymore, I'm the girl you called and cursed out, remember?"

"Anyways girl I'm back, this chick over here starting some drama."

She went back on her phone and rolled back up her window.

"Bitch you better move your damn car before I make sure you can't move!" Okay she just wants to ignore me so I went back inside for my pocket knife to stab up all her tires so I can really fuck her up. Mom and Joe came running behind me. "Phylisia what are you doing, you better stop!"

"Joe you better tell your bitch to wait for you across the street or I will fuck up all her damn tires, who the fuck you think you are bringing her here!"

"Alright I talk to her."

It didn't take long for his ass to run over by the car to let his chick know what was up.

"Baby, you have to move your car because this girl is crazy she would fuck up all your tires."

"Okay baby anything for you."

I wasn't jealous it's just that I don't like nobody disrespecting me like that, wouldn't you? Then on top of everything I know he did this on purpose, son of a bitch! I hope he doesn't think I did that for him. All that drama I had to relax my mind, so I went back to mom's house. Now I can say it's really over look how fast he moved on he must have been had her. A couple of hours later I heard mom's mouth. "See you, Phylisia you love embarrassing people! Why in the hell you choose to come up to my job with all those excitement!"

"Well then mother if your ass wouldn't be doing his hair all of that wouldn't had happen."

Then out of nowhere "pop" she gave me a punch right on my right eye.

"You get the hell out! After I'm the one paying your damn bills, and rent! So you don't tell me what to do!"

I know what she did was wrong I have a right to be upset, once it's over in your daughter's eyes is should be over in her family's eyes too. To me that should be common sense but I guess every family is different. I didn't have any more to say but to get out, good thing it was the weekend so I choose to let Kamari stay.

My eye was feeling so swollen, it was tender I was hoping by tomorrow it will feel better. Waking up the next morning I couldn't believe it! I was only looking out of my left eye, I had to feel if my right eye was there. This shit is so fucking scaring I had to dial 911.

"Hello I know this will sound stupid but I can only see out of my left eye, I'm blind in one eye!"

"Okay meme just calm down an ambulance trunk is on their way."

Oh god I hope this is curable, like a punch can cause all of this? On my way to the hospital it was so uncomfortable not seeing anything on my right side. My mom ended up coming in, look like the doctor called her.

"Oh I'm so sorry, you know I didn't mean to."

Guess she was scared about what's going to happen because sorry is a word she doesn't use.

"Okay Ms. Phylisia you have a severe blood clot in your pupil, you will be just fine I'm going to prescribe you some eye drops to help it clear up fast, looks like you fell on something real hard."

Looking at mom with tears in her eyes I just had to agree with him. The way mom look relief she made sure to show her appreciation.

"Thank you, Doctor I will make sure I will take good care of her."

Yea let's hope she's telling the truth. Again I was back at mom's house, it took a good 23 weeks for my eye to clear up. While everything else was just getting worse, I found out my roommate moved out. Then mom was telling me I had no choice but to move back in because she couldn't afford the rent by herself. Living back home I didn't know want to do I couldn't trust what was going to happen next between us, but as usual I had no other choice.

"Dear God"

God I'm still sad

No matter what I try to do a smile can never last long on my face

I try…I try so hard

But these tears won't dry on my face

I know you telling me to "never give up"

But deep down inside I wish I can

I heard you said there's always somebody out there that has it worse

The only thing about that is I just haven't met that person as yet

You said that sometimes you have to ride the rough road before you ever reach the smooth

But I'm still waiting to see the smooth

Just remember…I'm still waiting to see the smooth

"You Have the Right to Remain Silent"

I stayed with mom for a good couple of weeks with no drama. Joe and I was over, plus he was expecting his own baby soon. The only sad part is he decided to deported himself and go back to Jamaica. He told my mom I was the reason why he was here, so without me he doesn't want to stay in America no more. Nights I do cry missing him but with all his criminal records I know it's going to be hard for him to come back. Living back home with my family was a lot of work but I can't lie when it comes to helping me out with Kamari that wasn't a problem. Everything was just back to normal, including hearing mom's mouth almost every day. Kamari was turning the big 1 years old so we were all planning his first birthday party. I was happy but deep down inside I was really disappointed of myself. I never wanted him to have a life like this, like look at me I'm here living underneath some one's roof in which he doesn't have his own room.

His birthday party was here and the amount of people that was here I made sure I kept a smile on my face. Oh look at him enjoying himself as usual he loves being the center of attention.

"Everybody come on its time to cut the cake."

I can't lie the way mom was so proud of how big he has gotten you would of swore it's her son. Just thinking about it might as well you say that after all she's the one who been really taking care of him.

"Happy birthday to you, happy birthday to you, happy birthday to Kamari, happy birthday to you…"

Looking at him so happy, and mom over there smiling and taking pictures feeling proud of what she overcome, I couldn't hold it in anymore I had to run to the bathroom. All I could do is cry I don't have anything, no money, no job not even my own bed to sleep in.

"Phylisia, Phylisia open the door it's me, Kelly-Ann."

I knew she would come to check up on me, out of everybody she's the one that will show concern. So I had no choice but to let her in.

"Come on in and lock the door behind you."

"Phylisia I know you're in a lot of pain right now, and I do understand why but don't let everyone see that, so just dry up your face and let's go out there like nothing just happen."

Basically she wants me to build up a wall in front of these people, like that's something new. So I went straight to the CD player to start playing back the music. Regardless of how I felt I know everybody enjoyed their self which was all that really matter.

All of this have me craving for something to drink which means I'm going out after this. So I made sure to hit some nigga up.

"Hey boo."

"What's up Slim what you up to for tonight?"

"Nothing are you coming to pick me up?"

"Yea, so go get ready."

"Alright, then." Just like that...see that's why it's good to have male friends. I waited until Kamari fell asleep then I was good to go. We ended up going to a couple of reggae spots and knowing me I couldn't party without a drink in my hand. Coming home it was around 6 in the morning I happen to went straight to bed. Right when sleep was going on good I happen to hear you know who's mouth. "See you Phylisia! I'm tired of you going out with different, different man and when you come home you just sleep through the whole day like you don't have anything to do!"

Okay here we go again, soon as she walks in she made sure she attacks me. "Mom what are you talking about, yes I went out so what's the problem."

"What's the problem? I like the fact the you can sleep but when it comes to me getting any sleep after I'm the one taking care of everyone in this damn house!"

"See when you talk like that I can't stand it, then you be wondering why I be leaving the house most of the time!"

Out of nowhere here comes Darian, my step brother who decided to give me a push against the door.

"Don't be talking to mom like that and she's the one taking care of your son!" After hearing that I had no choice but to fight back, who the fuck asks him for his damn opinion!

Like was that supposed to make me feel good?

"Both of you, stop! I'm going to call the cops!"

When I see her pick up the phone to call the cops Kelly-Ann and I ran out the back door, because I didn't want shit to do with them!

"Hold it! Freeze! Now slowly walk back inside with your hands up!"

Walking back inside all I can think is: Wow! Look how fast they ass choose to come, I bet if it was something serious they wouldn't have come this quick. There were two cops, both was white. One of them went upstairs to talk to mom and the other one was downstairs talking to me.

"Okay ma'am so your saying your mom and you were arguing then out of nowhere your stepbrother starting fighting you?"

"Yes sir, that's exactly what happen."

Right when I was talking to the cop his partner came and interrupted,

"Ma'am would you like to sit down?"

"Oh no thank you, I'm fine."

Then just when I was going to finish telling the story I felt the officer grab my arm and through me down on the floor.

"Well then you're under arrest!"

"What! How the fuck is you going to arrest me just because I didn't want to sit down, it's not like you told me to sit down! No instead you ask me your dumb ass motherfucker!"

I didn't care anymore what type of racist shit is that all I could do is curse their asses out. Sitting in the back seat of a cops' car looking at mom I knew she didn't know it would go this far, I know she learn her lesson again and of course it had to be by me. The main shit that was on my mind is I wanted to know what charge they were going to give me. I know there isn't no law stating if you don't want to sit down in your own place you can be arrested.

This is so fuck up!

Guess there's a new law in town that states if I'm not in your shade of color then my rights doesn't exist. All I have to say is...stick around because we will see about this, oh yes we will see.

"Lock Up"

I'm looking around why am I here?

Now this is the reason why good girls go bad

In their eyes I'm just like the others, a criminal

But when they looking for the real ones it's so hard for them to find

Then on top of all of that

You have people staring you down, watching your every move

All I have to say is that the people I'm watching is the same people who brought me here

And I can't get out because I'm…. Lock Up!

TO BE CONTINUED…….

Made in the USA
Charleston, SC
22 March 2016